in the beginning
Genesis 1 – 4
by Roger Fawcett

Series Editor: Tim Chester

THE
GoodBook
COMPANY

In the beginning: Genesis 1-4
A good book guide
© Roger Fawcett/The Good Book Company, 2010.

Published by
The Good Book Company
Tel (UK): 0845-225-0880
Tel (int) + (44) 208 942 0880
Email: admin@thegoodbook.co.uk

Websites
UK & Europe: www.thegoodbook.co.uk
N America: www.thegoodbook.com
Australia: www.thegoodbook.com.au
New Zealand: www.thegoodbook.co.nz

ISBN: 9781907377112

Printed in India

CONTENTS

Introduction: Good Book Guides

Every Bible-study group is different—yours may take place in a church building, in a home or in a cafe, on a train, over a leisurely mid-morning coffee or squashed into a 30-minute lunch break. Your group may include new Christians, mature Christians, non-Christians, mums and tots, students, businessmen or teens. That's why we've designed these *Good Book Guides* to be flexible for use in many different situations.

Our aim in each session is to uncover the meaning of a passage, and see how it fits into the "big picture" of the Bible. But that can never be the end. We also need to appropriately apply what we have discovered to our lives. Let's take a look at what is included:

⊕ **Talkabout:** most groups need to "break the ice" at the beginning of a session, and here's the question that will do that. It's designed to get people talking around a subject that will be covered in the course of the Bible study.

⊕ **Investigate:** the Bible text for each session is broken up into manageable chunks, with questions that aim to help you understand what the passage is about. **The Leader's Guide** contains **guidance on questions**, and sometimes ☑ additional "follow-up" questions.

☺ **Explore more (optional):** these questions will help you connect what you have learned to other parts of the Bible, so you can begin to fit it all together like a jig-saw.

⊖ **Apply:** As you go through a Bible study, you'll keep coming across **apply** sections. These are questions to get the group discussing what the Bible teaching means in practice for you and your church. ⊡ **Getting personal**, is an opportunity for you to think, plan and pray about the changes that you personally may need to make as a result of what you have learned.

⊕ **Pray:** We want to encourage prayer that is rooted in God's word—in line with His concerns, purposes and promises. So each session ends with an opportunity to review the truths and challenges highlighted by the Bible study, and turn them into prayers of request and thanksgiving.

The **Leader's Guide** and introduction provide historical background information, explanations of the Bible texts for each session, ideas for **optional extra** activities, and guidance on how best to help people uncover the truths of God's word.

Why study *Genesis*?

"In the beginning God created the heavens and the earth."
Genesis 1 v 1

We all like to know where we have come from. Our origins are the foundation of our identity and individuality. So we often introduce ourselves to people by mentioning not only our name but also where we are from: "Hi, I'm Jeff, from Stockport". This is often followed up fairly quickly by a comment about our job, or the fact that we are retired or looking for work.

But as Christians we should perhaps think about changing the way we do this. After all, our identity is in Christ now that we are saved. And our origins lie in God. That's what Genesis 1 – 4 is all about—our origins. The writer recorded these chapters, guided by the Holy Spirit, in order to teach us about God and His wonderful creation of the world. Maybe we should introduce ourselves like this: "Hi, I'm Jeff, a unique creation made in the image of God, and a fallen sinner who has been saved by Christ". It might lead to some interesting conversations!

The first few chapters of Genesis have drawn more attention and controversy than many other parts of the Bible. Christians and non-Christians alike read these chapters for information about the world. Consequently, there are many different interpretations. Most of us have probably had a conversation about how the world began. Even among Christians there are many differences of opinion. At best these lead to healthy debate, but at worst they can cause serious damage to relationships between Christian brothers and sisters.

However, the author didn't write these chapters to stir up controversy but to teach us about God. These studies aim to get to the heart of what the passage is saying about our Creator. Our goal must be to let the Bible passages set the agenda and to go where each chapter leads us, rather than to come to them with our own convictions and try to get the Bible passage to fit. In this way we will learn some wonderful things about God and perhaps some surprising things about His world.

Genesis 1 v 1-25
GOD CREATES

⊕ talkabout

1. What do you like to do that is creative? Music, cooking, sport?

We can all be very creative at times, but none of us can create a universe out of nothing. But God can. You may be very familiar with this passage of the Bible. If so, pray now that God will help you to see the truths in it once again.

⊥ investigate

> **Read Genesis 1 v 1-2**

2. What does verse 1 tell us about how the universe was made?

3. What was the world like before God set to work on it?

➔ apply

4. Think of people you know who are atheists, or who live without any thought or knowledge of God. Compare the life of someone who truly believes these opening verses of the Bible. What differences might you expect to see?

⊡ getting personal

Is the way you live your life any different from someone who believes that the universe came about through blind chance? How might someone realise, from watching the way you live, that you believe God created the universe? How quickly would that become clear?

⊥ investigate

> Read Genesis 1 v 3-13

5. Fill in days 1-3 in the table below.

Day	Formed	Day	Filled
1		4	
2		5	
3		6	

> **Read Genesis 1 v 14-25**

6. Now fill in days 4-6. These three days tell us how God *filled* the earth.

7. What is the recurring pattern in the account of each day?
   List all the phrases that are repeated in these verses.

   •

   •

   •

   •

   •

8. What is God's conclusion about all that He has made?

⊡ **explore more**

Read **Job 38 v 1-11**; **40 v 1-14**; **42 v 1-6**. (If you have time, read the whole of these chapters.)
When Job truly understands that God is the only One who has created the universe from nothing, how does he see himself and how does he respond to God?

⊡ apply

9. What is your overall reaction to this passage? In what ways might you be tempted to doubt God's word here?

10. What is your conclusion about creation? How similar is it to God's?

- How is our belief or doubt reflected in the way we live?

⊡ getting personal

How do you need to change your view of God's power after reading about His amazing creation?

How do you need to change your view about God's good design for life, the universe and everything?

⊡ pray

- Thank and praise God that He is a powerful Creator, and pray that you will live in the light of that truth.

- Ask Him for help to trust that His design is good.

2

Genesis 1 v 26 – 2 v 3
GOD RELATES

⊕ talkabout

1. List five things that you think make you distinctly "you".

-
-
-
-
-

- Why have you chosen these things in particular?

⊕ investigate

❯ Read Genesis 1 v 26-28

These verses tell us a lot about what it means to be human. Humans are put at the top spot of creation in Genesis 1. In this session we look at what sets us apart from the rest of creation. God relates to humans in a special way, but that privilege comes with special responsibilities.

2. List what God does in v 26-28 as He creates the first humans.

-
-
-

3. What are we told about what humans are like?

⟶ apply

4. Why should we view each human as unique and valuable? And why should we treat men and women as equal?

• How and why are these standards under attack today?

⊡ explore more

optional

Read **Psalm 8**, where David describes God's good design for humankind.

• How does David show the insignificance of humans here?
• How does he show the glory of humans?
• How do humans compare with God?
• How are humans to relate to God?

Compare **Hebrews 2 v 6-9**. We have failed to rule as God designed (v 8) but what has Jesus Christ done to be crowned with glory and honour?

⊥ investigate

▶ Read Genesis 1 v 26 — 2 v 3

5. What instructions does God give humanity here?

-
-
-

6. What do these instructions imply about how humans are to relate to God?

• How are humans to relate to creation?

7. What do we learn about God in v 29-30?

8. What is God's conclusion about creation when it is finished (v 31)?

⊟ apply

9. What have you learned about God in these verses?

- How does this compare with views about God that are common today?

10. What makes a good ruler? And a bad one?

- What sort of "ruler" are you over God's creation—the environment, living creatures and other humans?

11. No one gets it right! We are all made in God's image but only Jesus Christ has ever "ruled" in the way that God intended at the beginning. How can you become more like Christ in the way you think and live? (See **Philippians 2 v 5-11** and **1 Peter 2 v 21-24**.)

⊕ pray

Say sorry...

• that you do not treat God's creation in the way He intended.

• that you do not get the relationships within creation right.

• that you have failed to relate rightly to your Creator.

Ask God to help you live according to His plan for creation...

• to show care for His world.

• to serve others as Jesus did.

• to gladly trust and obey Him.

3

Genesis 2 v 4-25

GOD PROVIDES

⊕ talkabout

1. Make a list of the things that all humans beings need—whether citizens in a modern technological culture or "stone-age" tribes from the jungle.

Genesis 2 is not "Creation: Take 2". It's the same act of creation from a different camera angle. In fact, it's a close-up, focusing on one part—the creation of humankind. Chapter 1 taught us that the entire universe is God's—He created it and it is good. In chapter 2 it is still God who is doing all the action. Adam and Eve are totally inactive. Watch out for the description of the wonderful world God created for men and women.

⊕ investigate

▶ **Read Genesis 2 v 4-25**

2. Fill in the table with the things that God provides for Adam.

	God provides:
Verse 7	
Verse 8	
Verse 9	
Verses 10-11, 13-14	
Verse 12	

	God provides:
Verse 15	
Verses 16-17	
Verses 18, 22	

• Does anything on the list surprise you?

3. What impression do verses 9-14 give of the Garden of Eden? (How did it compare with the rest of the earth—v 5?)

• What must it have been like to live in this garden?

4. What was the work the man was given in verse 15?

• How does this verse match the description in 1 v 28?

5. God also provides boundaries. What instructions does God give the man in verses 16-17?

• What's the balance here between freedom and restriction?

• Why does God have the right to make the rules in the Garden of Eden?

⮕ apply

When we think of God as our Provider, we may not automatically include work or His commands among the gifts for which we thank Him.

6. How could your attitude to work change in the light of Genesis 2 v 15?

7. How do you feel about being under God's rule? In which areas of your life do you need to change your attitude to God's authority over you?

☺ getting personal

Why not make it a particular project this week to thank God for things He provides that perhaps you are not always sufficiently thankful for— your everyday occupation maybe, or a command from God that you are struggling to obey?

⬇ investigate

8. One of God's most significant provisions for man is woman. Why did the man need the woman (v 18)?

• How are the animals *similar* to Adam? Why are they not suitable as his helper (v 19-20)?

• Why is the woman suitable (v 22-23)?

9. Compare the two accounts of the woman's creation in chapters 1 and 2 (1 v 26-28 and 2 v 18, 21-25). What things can we learn about women?

10. Summarise what v 18-24 tell us about God's design for the relationship between a man and a woman? See also:

• Matthew 19 v 1-6

• 1 Corinthians 11 v 3, 8

⮕ apply

11. What problems do people have today with God's good design for marriage and gender roles?

- How can you make sure you trust in God and live according to His good design? How can you avoid being tempted into harmful lifestyles or relationships?

optional

⊡ explore more

In the New Testament God provides even more for His people "in Christ". Look at the following Bible passages and complete the table.

	How has God provided for Christians?	What is the result for us?
1 Corinthians 1 v 7		
2 Corinthians 9 v 8		
Ephesians 1 v 3		
Philippians 4 v 19		
2 Peter 1 v 3		

What kind of lives will we live when we truly believe that this is how God provides for His people?

⊡ getting personal

Have you grasped how wonderful God's creation is? Is there anything that stops you trusting in His goodness? How do you need to change your response to God, in view of what you have learned about Him from creation?

⊙ pray

- Thank God that He is a God who provides. Thank Him for looking after His wonderful creation. Include something specific, mentioned in this session, that He has provided for you.

- Ask God to help you get your attitudes and relationships right, in line with His design. Most of all, ask Him to help you trust Him, even when you don't understand the reasons behind His good design.

Genesis 3 v 1-7

GOD RULES

⊕ talkabout

1. Think of people that you trust, or an occasion when you had to put total trust in someone. How did you come to trust in that person?

Genesis chapter 3 is actually about trust and obedience. Are Adam and Eve going to trust that God has got it right? Is His creation really "very good"? Are His rules fair? As you read the chapter, keep in mind that the wrong things we humans think and do (our sins) are caused by something deeper. It's our refusal to trust in God's word that leads to disobedience. That is our real rebellion.

⊕ investigate

❯ Read Genesis 3 v 1-7

2. What does the serpent first say to Eve (v 1)?

• How does he *begin* to tempt Eve to go against God's command?

3. How correct is Eve in her answer (v 2-3; compare 2 v 16-17)?

4. What suggestions does the serpent make about God in verses 4-5?

• In what way does he raise further doubts about God's word?

5. Having rejected God's word, how does Eve make her decision about the forbidden fruit (v 6)?

6. How does eating the fruit show us that Adam and Eve did not trust God?

⟶ apply

Eve fell into the serpent's trap because she didn't know God's word very well and she spent time listening to God's enemy.

7. How could you get to know God's word better?

8. In what ways do you listen to God's enemy?

• What do you need to do about that?

☺ explore more

optional

Read **Isaiah 44 v 24 – 45 v 14**. Here Isaiah is speaking about God's rule over Cyrus, the Persian emperor and the most powerful man on earth in his day.

- List all the things mentioned in these verses that God alone has the power and authority to do.

- How does Cyrus compare with the LORD?

- What is the main lesson for us here (45 v 5a and end of v 14)?

- What does that mean for us in practice (45 v 9-11)?

- What was Jesus' view of God's authority? Read **John 6 v 38**; **15 v 10**; **Philippians 2 v 5-8**; **1 Corinthians 15 v 22-28**.

⊻ investigate

9. After eating the forbidden fruit, Adam and Eve's eyes are opened (v 7). How do they react? (Compare 2 v 25.)

10. The man was given the job of ruling creation (see 1 v 28; 2 v 15), with the woman as his helper (2 v 20b-22). How has God's order in creation now been turned upside down?

➔ apply

11. In what areas of life do we find it particularly difficult to trust God?

• What have you learned so far in Genesis that will help you to trust God in these situations?

⊡ getting personal

Think about a situation where you find it particularly difficult to trust God and obey His word. What will you start doing from today to grow in trustful obedience to the Ruler of the universe?

⬆ pray

Ask God...

• to help you trust Him more, particularly in the situation highlighted by question 11.

• to help you live humbly under His word, even when you don't understand His reasons or you disagree with something He has said.

• to forgive you for the times when you do not trust in His goodness and you ignore His rule.

5

Genesis 3 v 8-24
GOD JUDGES

⊕ talkabout

1. Have you ever been punished for something? Was it fair or unfair of the person who punished you?

• What makes a punishment fair or unfair?

The second half of chapter 3 tells us about the necessary punishment that results from Adam and Eve's disobedience. Many people are surprised by the fact that God judges those who go against Him. But what should really shock us is sin and its results, especially when we look back at chapter 2 and remind ourselves of how perfect God's creation was.

⊕ investigate

❯ Read Genesis 3 v 8-13

2. What is Adam and Eve's reaction to God?

• What has changed from chapter 2?

3. What are Adam and Eve's excuses when God confronts them? Who blames who?

⊟ apply

4. Just as Adam and Eve tried to avoid responsibility, how do you play "the blame game" with sin?

• And how does guilt about sin affect your relationship with God?

⊡ getting personal

What is it at present that is making you feel ashamed—causing you to cover up, hide from God, and avoid blame? Read 1 John 1 v 8-9—God's promise to those who put their trust in Jesus Christ. Resolve to stop ignoring your sin, and instead let God deal with it as soon as possible.

⊌ investigate

▶ **Read Genesis 3 v 14-24**

5. What are the different curses that God gives?

• The serpent:

• Eve:

• The ground:

• Adam:

6. What is the final judgment on rebellion (v 23-4)?

• Why must Adam and Eve be punished in this way (v 22)?

7. There is a ray of hope. What is being predicted in the last part of v 15? Which offspring of a woman will one day crush the serpent—Satan? (See Hebrews 2 v 14.)

8. In spite of His punishment, what shows that God would continue to care and provide for His creation (v 21)?

• What would God's provision not do for the man and woman at this stage?

Read **Psalm 50**.

- What do we learn here about God's nature and character (v 1-15)?
- What examples of wickedness does God highlight (v 16-20)?
- Why must God punish wickedness (v 21)?
- How does God also show mercy (v 23)?
- How does Psalm 50 fit with what we have already learned in Genesis 1 – 3?

⊡ apply

9. How do the events of Genesis 1 – 3 explain the way our world is today?

10. How would you answer someone who questions whether God is right and fair to punish sin?

⊡ getting personal

Look at what has happened to the wonderful creation of chapter 2. How big an impact has reading these two chapters together had on you? Do you begin to feel the tug of losing God's perfect place and the horror of living in a world full of sin?

⊡ pray

Ask God to help you trust that His judgment of sin is right and just.

Thank God...

- that He continues to provide for His creation, even though we have rebelled against Him.
- for the hope there is in this passage—that sin can be defeated and Satan crushed.

6 Genesis 4 v 1-26
GOD REMAINS

⊕ talkabout

1. What are your hobbies? Are you any good at them?
(Don't be humble!) Would your friends say something different?

• Have you ever achieved anything with your hobbies eg: a prize in a show or a picture in the newspaper?

Chapter 4 v 1-2 seems to continue the story of 1 v 28—Adam and Eve have children and the first family begins to look after God's world. But then there's trouble—relationships between people, God and the world seem to be straining and beginning to crack.

The shadow of chapter 3 looms over chapter 4. A distance now exists between man and God. People try to devise their own ways to replace what they are now missing because of their separation from God—people try religion, technology and culture as routes to fulfilment.

⊕ investigate

> **Read Genesis 4 v 1-16**

2. What are the similarities and differences between the two brothers' offerings?

	What they offered	How God reacted
Abel		
Cain		

3. What clues are there as to why Cain's offering was rejected?

• What does **Hebrews 11 v 4** tell us about Abel's sacrifice?

4. How do you think Cain expected God to respond to his offering, and why?

• What was wrong with his thinking? (See Luke 18 v 9-14.)

5. What choice and consequences did God set before Cain (v 6-7)?

• What do you think "doing right" would involve for Cain?

6. What are the results of Cain's sinful offering? What do you notice about how sin spreads and grows (v 7-12)?

7. But how does God show mercy even to Cain (v 13-16)?

⊖ apply

Presumption and familiarity seem to be part of Cain's problem. He presumes that his sacrifice will be accepted, yet he has become sloppy in what he offers to God. Perhaps he has also become over-familiar with God, and doesn't respect God's holiness highly enough. In his decision-making, Cain thinks he knows better than God.

8. In what ways are we likely to become over-familiar or presumptive in our worship of God, both as individuals and as a church?

• How do you think God views hasty, careless worship?

⊡ getting personal

Worship is something that encompasses our whole lives, not just the hour that we spend singing together on Sunday. How can you "do what is right" and offer a humble and acceptable sacrifice of your own life? (See Romans 12 v 1-2.) How can you encourage other Christians to respect God's holiness with honour?

⊡ explore more

optional

Read **1 Kings 18 v 16-38**. Elijah's confrontation with the prophets of Baal—or, more accurately, the showdown between God and the false god, Baal—teaches us a lot about worship and prayer. The prophets of Baal could only try to cajole their non-existent "god" into action with ever increasing fervour. They believed that if they became more frantic and extreme, Baal would be duty bound to answer. They were wrong – see verse 29.

• How does Elijah's prayer contrast with the prophets' worship (v 36-37)?

• What does Elijah appeal to and what is his desire?

• How might we treat God in a way that is similar to the prophets' worship of Baal? (See also **Matthew 6 v 5-8**.)

• What can we learn from Elijah that will help us avoid this?

⬇ investigate

> **❯ Read Genesis 4 v 17-26**

9. What are some of the great achievements of these pioneers of the human race?

• Jabal:

• Jubal:

• Tubal-Cain:

10. How successful (or not) are these achievements in solving mankind's predicament resulting from the fall?

• What is the evidence here that humanity's problem is insoluble? (Think about Lamech in v 23-24.)

11. How does this chapter end with a note of hope (25-26)?

⊖ apply

Genesis 1 – 4 does more than merely explain our existence. It provides the foundation for understanding the rest of the Bible. We have seen that God made the world, that He rules and that He is good. But this world is now fallen and frustrated. God's rule is opposed; so punishment, death and exile inevitably follow. The rest of the Bible is the story of how God will resolve the seemingly impossible situation of restoring His world and His people.

12. Since we *cannot* bridge the gap between God and us by our own efforts, what needs to happen to restore us to a right relationship with our creator?

⊡ getting personal

Do you recognise times in your life when sin has been "crouching at the door" and threatening to trap you. Perhaps this is happening to you right now? What can you do at these times? What practical steps will you take to make sure that you do not fall into its clutches?

In what ways are you tempted to glorify your own achievements? How can the lessons of Genesis 4 help you get a better perspective on this impulse?

⬆ pray

Genesis chapter 4 should cause us to mourn the loss of Eden and realise that we cannot rebuild our relationship with God from our side. Talk to God about that now.

• Ask God to help you speak to others about Him, especially those who are relying on their own abilities and ignoring His grace.

John 1 v 1-14
GOD STEPS IN

⊕ talkabout

1. Look back at the studies so far and pick out some of the highlights of the things you have learned. What have you discovered so far about Jesus?

We have seen that God has created a wonderful world that has been ruined by sin. Nothing we can do is able to cross the gap that sin has created between God and us. God needs to step in and cross the gap from His side. Wonderfully, God does this through Jesus, to whom John gives the title "the Word".

⊕ investigate

❯ Read John 1 v 1-2

2. What do you notice about the first few words of John's Gospel? They should remind you of something.

3. The Word is Jesus. What do these two verses tell us about who Jesus is and what He is like?

▶ Read John 1 v 3-5

4. What do these verses tell us about the part Jesus played in creation?

5. What else does Jesus bring into the world?

optional

⊡ **explore more**

Check out the presence of the Trinity at Jesus' baptism (**Matthew 3 v 16-17**), or in Jesus' blessing in the "Great Commission" (**Matthew 28 v 16-20**) or in the amazing description of what it means to be a Christian in **Ephesians 1 v 1-14**.

⊖ **apply**

6. It's hard to get our heads round the fact that Jesus is God and yet He is separate from God the Father. Why is it important to believe this?

�↓ **investigate**

▶ Read John 1 v 6-9

7. What was the role of John the Baptist? What was the very exciting event that he was looking forward to?

> **Read John 1 v 10-13**

8.   What are the two reactions to Jesus' presence in the world?

• How can we become "children of God"?

• When that happens what difference does it make, do you think?

> **Read John 1 v 14**

9.   What has Jesus—"the Word"—done?

• What does Jesus reveal to us by doing this?

⤳ apply

It is absolutely right to conclude these studies in Genesis by challenging ourselves about our response to God the Creator. John has shown us that this means our response to Jesus.

10. What beliefs and actions would you expect to see in someone who claims to recognise who Jesus is and to have "received" Him?

getting personal

Creation belongs to God. After all these studies what do you most need to change in your life to accept God's rule?

Through Jesus the gap between God and man has been bridged. The glory of God in Eden is accessible to us once more when we receive Christ. In what areas of your life do you still need to accept Jesus' rule?

⬆ pray

- In your prayers acknowledge Jesus as your Creator and thank Him for sending Jesus into the world to cross that gap between us and God.

- Look back through these studies in Genesis and thank God for what you have learned. In your prayers commit yourself to live in the light of what you have learned.

in the beginning
Genesis 1 – 4

LEADER'S GUIDE

Leader's Guide: In the beginning

Introduction

Leading a Bible study can be a bit like herding cats—everyone has a different idea of what the passage could be about, and a different line of enquiry that they want to pursue. But a good group leader is more than someone who just referees this kind of discussion. You will want to:

- **correctly understand** and handle the Bible passage. But also…

- **encourage and train** the people in your group to do this for themselves. Don't fall into the trap of spoon-feeding people by simply passing on the information in the Leader's Guide. Then…

- make sure that no Bible study is finished without everyone **knowing how the passage is relevant for them**. What changes do you all need to make in the light of the things you have been learning? And finally…

- encourage the group to turn all that has been learned and discussed into **prayer**.

Your Bible-study group is unique, and you are likely to know better than anyone the capabilities, backgrounds and circumstances of the people you are leading. That's why we've designed these guides with a number of optional features. If they're a quiet bunch, you might want to spend longer on **talkabout**. If your time is limited, you can choose to skip **explore more**, or get people to look at these questions at home. Can't get enough of Bible study? Well, some Guides have optional extra homework projects. As leader, you can adapt and select the material to the needs of your particular group.

So what's in the Leader's Guide?

The main thing that this Leader's Guide will help you to do is to understand the major teaching points in the passage you are studying, and how to apply them. As well as guidance on the questions, the Leader's Guide for each session contains the following important sections:

THE BIG IDEA

One key sentence will give you the main point of the session. This is what you should be aiming to have fixed in people's minds as they leave the Bible study. And it's the point you need to head back towards when the discussion goes off at a tangent.

SUMMARY

An overview of the passage, including plenty of useful historical background information.

OPTIONAL EXTRA

Usually this is an introductory activity, that ties in with the main theme of the Bible study, and is designed to "break the ice" at the beginning of a session. Or it may be a "homework project" that people can tackle during the week.

So let's take a look at the various features of a Good Book Guide.

⊕ **talkabout**: each session kicks off with a discussion question, based on the group's opinions or experiences. It's designed to get people talking and thinking in a general way about the main subject of the Bible study.

⊕ **investigate**: the first thing that you and your group need to know is what the Bible passage is about, which is the purpose of these questions. But watch out—people may come up with answers based on their experiences or teaching they have heard in the past, without referring to the passage at all. It's amazing how often we can get through a Bible study without actually looking at the Bible! And if you're stuck for an answer, the Leader's Guide contains guidance on questions. These are the answers to which you need to direct your group. This information isn't meant to be read out to people—ideally, you want them to discover these answers from the Bible for themselves. Sometimes optional follow-up questions (see ☑ in "guidance on questions") are included, to help you help your group get to the answer.

⊞ **explore more**: these questions generally point people to other relevant parts of the Bible. They are useful for helping your group to see how the passage fits into the "big picture" of the whole Bible. These sections are **OPTIONAL**—only use them if you have time. Remember—it's better to finish in good time having really grasped one big thing from the passage, than to try and cram everything in.

➔ **apply**: we want to encourage you to spend more time working at application—too often, it is simply tacked on at the end. In the **Good Book Guides**, apply sections are mixed in with the investigate sections of the study. We hope that people will realise that application is not just an optional extra, but rather, the whole purpose of studying the Bible. We do Bible study so that our lives can be changed by what we hear from God's word. If you skip the application, the Bible study hasn't achieved its purpose.

These questions draw out practical lessons that we can all learn from the Bible passage. You can review what has been learned so far, and think about practical differences that this should make in our churches and our lives. The group gets the opportunity to talk about what they personally have learned.

⊡ **getting personal** can be done at home, or you could allocate a few moments of quiet reflection for each person to think about specific changes that they need to make and pray through in their own lives.

Why not have a time for reporting back at the beginning of the following session, so that everyone can be encouraged and challenged by one another to make application a priority?

⊕ **pray**: In Acts 4 v 25-30 the first Christians quoted Psalm 2 as they prayed in response to the persecution of the apostles by the Jewish religious leaders. Today however, it's not as common for Christians to base prayers on the truths of God's word as it once was. As a result, our prayers tend to be weak, superficial and self-centred rather than bold, visionary and God-centred.

The prayer section is based on what has been learned from the Bible passage. How different our prayers would be if we were genuinely responding to what God has said to us through His word.

Introduction to Genesis 1 – 4

The aim of this Good Book Guide is to teach the central theme of each Bible passage and let God's word decide what's important. If you are leading a Bible study on these chapters, resist the temptation, and perhaps pressure from some members of your group, to launch off into technical discussion on the big bang, evolutionary theory, fossils, environmental issues, or even sex and marriage. Although you and others in the group may be hungry to know the answers to these questions, and have strong opinions about them, there is a real danger that these discussions are a distraction, and take us away from listening to the powerful things God is saying to us.

Remember that these issues are largely modern questions that were not current when Genesis was first written, so, although what is taught in these early chapters of Genesis may have some implications for these subjects, they cannot be the main focus of their message.

Allow the Bible to set the agenda and have its impact. Other issues can be followed up later once the right foundations have been properly built.

Genesis 1 - 4 acts as an introduction to the whole Bible, showing us whose world it is and who is in control. We are introduced to life as it should be—in God's wonderful garden, with perfect friendship with God. We can feel the devastating impact of sin entering this perfect world and the enormous loss of that great existence in the garden. And these chapters show us the beginning of the spiral of sin that soon goes out of control as evil sets its mark on the world and men fumble in vain to reach out for God.

Bear in mind that we are examining God's blueprint for life and relationships in these early chapters of Genesis. Chapters 1 and 2 show us God's good design for life—the way it was meant to be. Chapters 3 and 4 show the breakdown and consequences that come from rebelling against His will. This will become important later as we refer back to God's good design, in order to set the scene for issues that are raised elsewhere in the Bible.

The final study takes us to where this perfect, but fallen and now futile creation is redeemed—the coming of Christ into the world to reverse the curse that the fall brought upon humanity, and to open the way to God's new creation—Eden restored.

Bear in mind also that this set of Bible studies cannot do *everything* that comes out of these chapters. Because they are foundational for the whole of the Bible, a vast array of important subjects are touched: the pattern for marriage; our attitude to culture; law; the Sabbath rest; the environment etc.

This Good Book Guide has deliberately focused on trying to follow the plotline of salvation in the Bible and seeing how our understanding of these chapters is essential for understanding the whole message of the Bible. In that sense, this book is a primer for studying a part of the Bible from which you will be able to go on mining jewels for years to come.

Genesis 1 v 1-25
GOD CREATES

THE BIG IDEA

God created everything out of nothing and His design is good.

SUMMARY

Genesis chapter 1 is a very familiar passage of the Bible. It is often referred to and studied. But this is not an apology for starting at the very beginning. We need to start here in order to build up the picture of our world that the Bible has, and in order to read it and receive the same impact that the original readers felt.

The aim of this session is to see that it is God's world, that He made it and that it is good. The phrase "God's good design" could summarise what Genesis 1 is teaching. If we don't get hold of the fact that God's original design was good, we will never understand what follows about the fall, and God's plan of salvation.

This session also confronts us with the practical implications of the truth that God created the universe out of nothing. We cannot with integrity claim to believe this and yet continue to live just like everyone else around us.

OPTIONAL EXTRA

Read out a concise version of one or more creation myths (for example, see the "creation myths" entry in Wikipedia).

If your group know the story of creation in Genesis 1, get them to point out the important differences between a myth and the Bible's account. If people are new to the story of creation, encourage them to look out for the differences as you work through the session, and briefly review these before you finish. Here are some key points found in Genesis 1.

- In the beginning God already exists. He doesn't come into being.

- Matter doesn't pre-exist God: God pre-exists matter.

- The sun, moon, stars, sea, weather, animals etc. are things created by God, not deities with creative powers.

- God has complete power over creation. He sets boundaries, roles and laws. Nothing rivals him in power or authority.

- The creation of human beings is not an accident, or an afterthought of the gods, or something done merely to satisfy a divine whim. They are central to creation and the world is created for their use, care and benefit.

- The Genesis account describes the origins of the whole world and all its people. It does not seek to explain or validate a particular people, culture or local religion.

(Idea taken from *Salvation Begins* by Andrew Reid, p6-7)

GUIDANCE ON QUESTIONS

1. This question is an ice-breaker, exploring the idea of creativity at the beginning of a session which focuses on God's supreme and unique creativity in bringing the universe into existence out of nothing. The meaning of "creative" can be expanded so that non-artistic types needn't feel they are missing out—creativity isn't limited only to artistic endeavours.

2. Verse 1 tells us simply that God created the universe. "Heavens" here means everything from the ground upwards (rather than the spiritual realm), and "earth" means everything under our feet. So "heavens and earth" = the whole universe.

3. Verse 2 tells us that the earth was formless, empty and dark. This indicates that God didn't create our world instantaneously (see questions 5 and 6 below, on how God "formed" and "filled" the universe).

4. APPLY: How we understand our origins has a profound effect on how we view ourselves and our lives. A belief in the creatorship of God (not necessarily Christian faith) can make a practical difference in many areas of life such as marriage and other commitments, ambitions and priorities, our response to disappointments or troubles etc.

People who believe in a divine creator may also believe… that there is a purpose in life; that there are moral absolutes; that we are morally accountable for the way we live; that there are more important things in life than "my own happiness"; that history is moving purposefully towards a destiny; that we can pray and worship and are cared for by someone far greater than ourselves.

By contrast, the person who ignores or disbelieves in a divine creator will tend to… make up their own standards of right and wrong; believe that here and now is all we have, and will be motivated to get the very best for themselves out of this life; believe they must rely on themselves; see history as meaningless and death as final, and argue that accepting this bleak outlook is a sign of maturity; be very tolerant of other beliefs and lifestyles because they have no belief in absolute right and wrong; or conversely may live by the maxim "Might is right".

Note: Of course, on both sides of this divide there are people who do not live consistently with their beliefs eg: the atheist who believes in destiny, or the religious person who actually worships money and success.

5 and 6.

Day	Formed	Day	Filled
1	Day and night	4	Sun, moon and stars
2	Waters and sky	5	Sea creatures and birds
3	Land and seas	6	Animals and humans

7. The recurring pattern shows us that there is order and control, highlighting the key points. The recurring phrases are:

- *"And God said 'Let there be…'"*—showing the method of creation out of nothing and the power of God's word.

- *"And it was so."*—again emphasising God's power and sovereignty over creation.

- *"And God called…"*—showing God's rule over creation (note that man will similarly rule when he names the animals in chapter 2).

- *"God saw that it was good"*—a value statement from the Creator on the created: it's a good creation.

- *"And there was evening, and there was morning…"*—showing us that creation is ordered and disciplined. The point of the days is also to lead into the idea of rest from the work of creation on the seventh day.

8. This question emphasises the point that God's design for creation is good. This will be very important to remember later on.

EXPLORE MORE

The poetry in these final chapters of Job powerfully conveys the majesty and wonder of the events that are recorded so simply and briefly in Genesis 1. See 40 v 3-5 and 42 v 1-6 for Job's response to God's extensive and detailed proclamation of His creatorship. Job realises he is unworthy before God—he cannot even speak (40 v 3-6). He realises God is sovereign and all-powerful (42 v 2), and that he is ignorant and has spoken out of turn (v 3). Job ends by despising himself and repenting of the way he has lived (v 6), even though we are told (1 v 1) that he was a man who was blameless and upright, who feared God and shunned evil.

- Have you ever seen God as Job comes to see Him in these verses (42 v 5)? Have you ever responded to Him as Job did?

- What does it mean for us to "repent" today? See Mark 1 v 15; Acts 20 v 21. We repent by believing in the good news of Jesus Christ and trusting in what He has done to save us from our sins.

9. APPLY: It is likely that some of your group will have questions about creation/evolution which they will raise at this point. However, this is a complex issue and a comprehensive discussion may well take more time than is available in the session. Probably the best approach is to briefly outline the view adopted for these studies (see appendix on p77-78). Note down specific questions and discuss them at the end of the session or arrange another time for this. You may also want to recommend books, talks or DVDs. See, for example, *Salvation Begins* by Andrew Reid, p.14-20.

10. APPLY: This question gives an opportunity to discuss the teaching point of this passage—namely, that all of creation is God's and originally it was all designed well. Genesis 1 leaves us in no doubt that God believed His creation was good. However, though we may think that we share God's conclusion about His creation, the way we live often shows that we doubt God's design is good.

- Our tolerance of sin and lack of interest in living life God's way—usually expressed in selfishness and the desire for self-rule—shows that we don't believe that what God planned and created originally was good. This unbelief will become apparent in the sessions about the "Fall" (Adam and Eve's rebellion against God and its consequences for creation). We cannot truly understand the terrible impact of the Fall if we doubt that God's design for creation was good.

The world is a good thing that has gone wrong, not a fundamentally bad thing. So, although abused and turned to evil, alcohol, food, sex, natural resources etc are all good things in themselves.

2

Genesis 1 v 26 – 2 v 3
GOD RELATES

THE BIG IDEA

God relates to humans in a unique way, but that privilege comes with special responsibilities—to show God's likeness and to rule over His creation in obedience to His commands.

SUMMARY

In these verses we come to the climax of God's creation—where God makes, blesses, instructs and provides for humanity, and then rests. Here we see God's good design for the human race. Men and women, out of all creation, occupy a unique position and are given a unique role. We are to show God's likeness—not to be totally like God, but in the way we rule the rest of creation, exercise creativity and have relationships, particularly between the two sexes.

But all this is to take place in the context of a right relationship with God: God loves us, rules us and provides for us—we lovingly obey and trust Him. This session looks at how all humans, apart from Jesus Christ, have failed to live according to God's good design. As a result, we abuse creation, mistreat one another and ignore, reject or relate wrongly to our Creator.

We also see what it means to live as Jesus Christ did—the only human who has ever perfectly fulfilled God's good design for humanity. Trust in God and obedience to Him now come through the gospel of Christ, which is the only way to be reconciled to the God who relates.

OPTIONAL EXTRA

Print up the lyrics of a popular utopian song. The most well-known and coherent of these is probably "*Imagine*" by John Lennon. Or you could use Michael Jackson's "*Heal the world*", (equally well-known maybe but less coherent!). At the beginning of the session, play the song as people read through the words. Then divide your group into twos or threes to discuss what's commendable about the song, but also where it falls down. If people know something about Lennon or Jackson, you could talk about the extent to which they lived or failed to live in the light of their own songs. At the end of the session, compare the solution offered by the song with what has been learned from God's good design for humanity (ie: we humans can only rule creation well when we relate rightly our Creator). This activity aims to highlight the key difference between popular ideas of how to make the world a better place, and God's revelation in Genesis.

GUIDANCE ON QUESTIONS

1. Use this discussion to celebrate the wonder and diversity of the creation of each individual. Don't spend too long—it could take all night!

2. God **speaks** (v 26), God **creates** (v 27) and God **blesses** (v 28). Notice how active God is in just these three verses.

• **What do you think this emphasises?** God's actions emphasise that humans are very much **created** beings, intentionally designed, planned and provided for by God—not the result of an accident, afterthought or sudden whim.

3. We are made in God's image (mentioned three times); we are **different** from the rest of creation (because of the special emphasis of these verses and because we are made to rule over the other animals); we are created as male and female; and we are **blessed** by God. You could use the following optional extra questions to look at these characteristics in more detail. ("Ruling" is covered in **Explore More** and questions 10 and 11 below.)

• **What does it mean that humans are made in God's image and what does it not mean?** Humans show what God is like in some ways—we are to rule, we are creative, we relate (see below)—but not in all ways. As we shall see, a fundamental error of Adam and Eve was to believe that they could and would become "like God"—3 v 5.

• **God created man male and female in His image (v 27). Why are humans better able to show God's likeness because there are two sexes?** Draw people's attention to the clue in v 26, where God speaks of Himself as "us". This shows what the rest of the Bible confirms—that the one God is more than one person. He is a Trinity. Relationship, therefore, lies at the heart of God's nature. A single person of either sex cannot show a likeness of God's nature as effectively as two people

of different sex, who are different but complementary.

4. APPLY: This question aims to help people see that the teaching of Genesis 1 is the only secure foundation for a high view of the value of human life. We should view every person as unique and valuable because each of us is made by God and in His image. And we should treat men and women as equal because both sexes are made equally in God's image. Make the equality point strongly at this stage, because later in chapter 2 we will see that there are distinct roles.

• Many people in modern society aspire to this high view of human life but because the teaching of the Bible has been downgraded these values are inevitably under attack. The value of a human life is no longer based on the fact that each person is created by and in the likeness of God. Instead that value must be based on something like a person's "normality", independence, usefulness, economic value, or even social background or racial origin. For example: the practice of aborting babies suspected to have disabilities shows that able-bodied people are valued more highly; throughout the news media, incidents involving people from our culture are consistently seen as more newsworthy than those involving people in poorer countries; the gender pay gap and the pressure on mothers, even single ones, to go out to work seems to indicate that we value far less the women whose work is raising and caring for children than those who take a "paid" job outside the home.

EXPLORE MORE

Psalm 8: David compares humanity with the vastness and power of the heavens and heavenly bodies to show how insignificant we are in the scale of God's creation (v 3-4). But he shows the glory of humanity by outlining the God-given role of humans in creation—to rule over nature (v 5-8). Yet it is clear that the supreme glory belongs to God alone, whose name is majestic in all the earth (v 1, 9), and whose glory is set above the heavens (v 1); by contrast, humanity is "lower than the heavenly beings" (v 5). We are to relate to God by glorifying His name (v 1, 9) and praising Him (v 2), and by marvelling at His goodness and care for humanity (v 4).

Hebrews 2 v 6-9: Jesus alone has been crowned with glory and honour because He alone has fulfilled God's design for humanity by His obedience to God, even to the point of suffering death (v 9; see also Philippians 2 v 5-11). Humanity can only rule properly as God designed by showing trusting obedience to God's rule over us (see question 11 below).

5. We are to be fruitful and to increase in number, to fill the earth and subdue it, and to rule over the other creatures (v 28).

6. Humans are to relate to God by obeying Him. We are His created beings and we are given God's instructions for living in God's world.

• However, *we are to rule over the rest of creation*. If people already know the story of the Fall, you could ask them the optional extra question below. Otherwise simply make the point to your group.

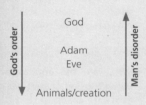

• **How does Eve re-order the hierarchy of relationships that God established?** Eve takes her orders from a snake—she is ruled by a creature; and she disobeys God—she refuses to be ruled by Him. You could sketch the diagram below to help people see this.

7. God provides for the needs not only of humanity but of all the creatures He has made. And He does this lavishly—notice the repeated use of the words "every" and "all" in these verses.

8. God concludes that His finished creation is not only good (see v 4, 10, 12, 18, 21, 25), but "very good".

9. APPLY: Review what you have learned in this session.

• God is the supreme ruler over His creation.

• He created humanity thoughtfully and intentionally to show His likeness to the rest of creation.

•• He has given us instructions to be obeyed.

• He has blessed us with lavish provision of everything we need.

• **What are the implications for us?** It is good to live under God's rule. We have a role to fulfil, a loving Ruler who gives us wise and good guidance to follow, and a Provider we can trust.

- Common views about God today include: that He is distant or dispassionate—uninterested and uninvolved in what we do; that He is a tyrant who stifles our freedom and judges us harshly and unfairly; that He is well-meaning but for whatever reason unable to help us and provide what we truly need.

⌄

- **What are the implications of these views?** If God doesn't get involved with humanity, there's no point in trying to have a relationship with Him; if God is a tyrant, people will fear Him, avoid Him, try to placate Him, or resent Him; if God is unable to help us, people won't trust Him but seek to take control of their own lives instead.

10. APPLY: Characteristics of bad rulers include: harsh, neglectful, unfair, self-interested, exploitative, abusive, uncompassionate, untrustworthy, deceitful, unprincipled, greedy, lazy etc. It may be easier for your group to identify what makes a bad ruler than a good one. You can use the opposites to build up a picture of a good ruler.

- This gives an opportunity to briefly discuss any need for change in the attitudes of churches and Christians to the care of the environment, living creatures and certain types of people, both in our communities (foreigners, the elderly, those living in areas of high social deprivation, the learning disabled, Muslims etc.) and beyond (the under-developed world).

11. APPLY: First you need to establish how Jesus Christ (the only perfect man—see Explore More above) "ruled" during His time on earth. Philippians 2 v 5-11 and 1 Peter 2 v 21-24 show that Christ served others—in fact, he suffered in His service of others. And He was able to do that because He trusted (1 Peter 2 v 23b) and obeyed (Philippians 2 v 8) God. This should lead into a discussion about areas in which we need to work on trusting God and obeying Him, both as individuals and as a church. For example… On the issue of trust: do we trust that God's word is all we—and the non-Christians around us—need to live as God designed us to (2 Timothy 3 v 16-17)? Do we trust that the gospel is for everyone and the only solution to their deepest needs? Do we trust that God can use each one of us, however weak or sinful we feel, in the work of bringing people to Jesus Christ to be saved? On the issue of obedience: are we obeying the "Great Commission" (Matthew 28 v 18-20)? Are we willing to suffer persecution and shame for the gospel, like Jesus and Paul?

⌄

- **What is the best way in which we can serve other people?** By helping people to hear the gospel—by sharing it with them, by demonstrating it with our lives, and by inviting and bringing them to events or groups where they will hear it.

3 Genesis 2 v 4-25
GOD PROVIDES

THE BIG IDEA

God has provided humanity with everything we need and all of it is good, so we should trust in His goodness and submit to His authority.

SUMMARY

Genesis 2 shows us how wonderful God's provision for humanity was. The Garden of Eden was a wonderful home for the first man and woman, full of food, beauty and scope for creativity and exploration. God also provided the man with work, instructions and a helper suitable for him—the first woman. Thus we learn about God's good design for human life. Genesis 2 reminds us of what life should be like, establishes man's role within creation, and sets down the pattern for relationships between men and women and for families.

Genesis 2 also shows us the nature and character of God. God's authority to rule His creation is unquestioned. But He is also seen to be lavishly generous and thoughtful of every need of humanity. This session provides the context for the Fall (man's rebellion against God—Genesis 3), the results of which will contrast starkly with the peace, security and richness of life in Eden.

This session encourages us to trust in the goodness of God, already seen in His good design for human life. We are challenged to

see God's design for work, boundaries and marriage as good and life-affirming gifts of our Creator, rather than chains on our freedom and threats to our happiness.

OPTIONAL EXTRA

(You'll need a roll of lining paper and a marker pen.) The aim of this activity is to help people appreciate God's sheer generosity in giving the first humans freedom to eat from any tree except one (2 v 16). Actually, it can be extended to all edible plants (see 1 v 29). Divide your group into twos or threes. Give each sub-group a few letters of the alphabet, so that the whole alphabet is allocated. Ask people to come up with a list of all the edible fruit, nuts, seeds and vegetables they can think of for their letters of the alphabet. Then, starting with the letter A, get people to call these out and write them down on the roll of paper. Or you could cut the roll into sections marked with the various letters, give one section to each sub-group to write on as they think of items, and stick the sections together at the end. The result should be a very long and impressive list of foods provided by God (and even this will only be a selection of what is available world-wide), and will provide a stark contrast with the single fruit that God forbade the man and woman to eat. (You could do this in conjunction with question 5.)

GUIDANCE ON QUESTIONS

1. The question specifies "all humans" so people shouldn't include things that are relevant only in the developed world eg: money, a car, electricity. Get people to compare their lists, see how much they agree and add in things mentioned by others that they haven't thought of. Answers might include: food and water, warmth and shelter, companionship, security from danger, health, resources, something to do with their time, a purpose in life, creativity, leisure and rest, enjoyment, rules and boundaries, a relationship with God. As you go through the session, encourage people to look out for the way in which God provides for these needs.

2.

	God provides
Verse 7	Life
Verse 8	A garden
Verse 9	Trees, beauty, food
Verses 10-11, 13-14	Water and irrigation
Verse 12	Minerals
Verse 15	Work/a job
Verses 16-17	Instructions/ a warning
Verses 18 & 22	A helper (the woman)

3. The Garden of Eden was specially prepared by God as a home for the first man and woman. God Himself planted trees there (v 8), whereas the rest of the earth was left bare, waiting for plants to grow by themselves (v 5). There was a great variety of trees, and God designed them to provide beauty as well as food (v 9). God provided abundant water (v 10) so that the garden would continue to flourish.

• Clearly, Eden was an attractive, abundant and fascinating place in which to live. There would be no shortage of food, so life would be comfortable. It was also enjoyable and interesting because of the variety of things that were "pleasing to the eye". God had already planted and grown the garden so there was no hard work to be done in turning it into a home.

4. The man was both to "work" the garden and to "take care of it". (You could ask your group how they might work a garden eg: digging, planting, weeding; and what they would do to take care of it eg: watering, feeding, protecting a worn lawn, leaving a vegetable patch fallow.) "Working" suggests active involvement eg: changing things, moving things, trying out different ideas etc. "Taking care" highlights the aim of the man's work. In modern terms, he was to use the garden in a way that was sustainable, and not exploitative. His work was not just for his own good but for the good of the garden.

• 2 v 15 isn't the first reference to work in Genesis. The idea of work is present in 1 v 28. Clearly, while Eden was a wonderful garden, it still needed "subduing".

☑

• **How might we understand working the earth and taking care of it today?** Get your group to think how 2 v 15 guides our response to the environmental debate. The fact that God designed the man to work the earth tells us that it's good for humans to interact with our physical and natural environment, and contradicts the more extreme environmentalists who argue for lifestyles to have minimal impact on our natural surroundings. On the other hand, the fact that we are to take care of the earth clearly suggests that we should avoid causing irreparable damage to the natural world and we should invest in restoring and repairing our environment.

5. In v 17, the man is given a single prohibition—not to eat from the tree of the knowledge of good and evil—and also clearly warned of the consequences if he disobeys. But the context of this prohibition is God's statement in v 16 that the man is free to eat from any other tree in the garden. (Note: You will probably need to explain what is meant by "the knowledge of good and evil". God prohibited Adam from eating the fruit of this tree to show that humans must not decide what is right (good) and wrong (evil) independently of God.)

- At this stage God has given humans almost total freedom. There is only one single prohibition to restrict that freedom. The truth about God in Genesis 2 is very different from today's popular view that He is a repressive and mean control-freak. (See Optional Extra above.)

- God is the Creator and we are His creation. Notice that no case is argued for God's right to make the rules—it is simply assumed. This might seem like an obvious question, but it is important to get this clear before considering the significance of man's rebellion at the Fall.

6. APPLY: Include unpaid everyday occupations (housewife, mum, grandparent, church volunteer etc) in your definition of "work". Our culture tends to view work at best as a necessary evil. Ask for examples of this (eg: dreams of winning the lottery

often involve giving up work; people "live for" the weekend and holidays; everyone knows what a "Monday morning feeling" is, etc). As we shall see, our experience of work has been blighted by God's curse on human sin (3 v 17-19). However, the fantasy that the perfect life is work free is not based on God's good design for humanity revealed here in Genesis 2. (**Pastoral note:** Be aware that some in your group may be finding work very stressful or depressing, and these problems should not be minimised or ignored. This question may bring some of these issues into the open and you should be prepared to offer extra support and encouragement outside the session.)

7. APPLY: As we shall see in Genesis 3, God's right to exercise authority over His creation is the key issue on which all humans since Adam and Eve have gone astray. If people don't think that this is true of them, check out 1 Peter 1 v 14-15. Discuss what are some of the evil desires that we had before becoming a Christian that we still struggle against now. You may need to begin with an example from your own life. Or give people a couple of minutes to write down the things that as yet they can't share, and then pray for each other.

8. Woman was created because "it is not good for man to be alone" (v 18)—for companionship and, in the context of this passage (v 24-25), marriage. The man needed "a helper suitable for him" (v 18), to carry out the role that God had given him.

- The animals are similar to the man in as much as they are formed in the same way (v 19a, compare v 7), but Adam's investigation of each one as part of the naming process still leads him to conclude that none of them is suitable to be his helper (v 20).

- The woman is suitable because she is like the man (v 23)

9. Women were created at the same stage of creation as men. They have also been created in God's image. (In fact, both male and female are needed to show God's likeness.) Therefore women have equal value with men in God's eyes. But as we shall see, they have a different role to men. This begins to be played out in chapter 2.

10. There are two aspects to consider in answering this question. **1. Marriage and family:** God's creation of the woman as a suitable helper for the man led to the institution of marriage (v 24-25). This was also commended by Jesus in Matthew 19 v 1-6, where he quotes from Genesis 2. Marriage, and the family life that develops from marriage, is good and godly. And marriage is the only model for human sexual relationships. **2. Headship:** (= a husband's authority over his wife). According to Paul in 1 Corinthians 11 v 3 and 8, God's good design in giving a husband authority over his wife is shown by the fact that the woman was created out of the man (Genesis 2 v 21-22) and for his benefit—to be his helper (v 18), rather than the other way round. (**Note:** The word "woman" in 1 Corinthians 11 v 3 can also be translated "wife" depending on the context, in which case the word "man" means "husband". This is how the ESV translates this verse and is the interpretation followed here.)

- **What should this mean in practice?** (See Ephesians 5 v 22-33. Try not to get too distracted from the main point of the session, which is to show all that God has provided for humanity (including the gift of marriage), rather than the detail of Bible teaching about male/female relationships, and the controversies that rage on this subject.)

11. APPLY: Briefly list the ways in which modern societies today have departed from God's good design for male/female relationships eg: moving on from one marriage/relationship to the next (serial monogamy); more than one partner at the same time (polygamy or philandering); same-sex sexual relationships; the rejection of male headship in marriage (reflected in modern marriage vows). Note that some traditional societies depart from God's good design for sexual relationships in different ways: most notably, by treating women as inferior to men, and by forcing wives to join their husband's family, rather than following God's pattern, where a man leaves his parents to get married. Discuss why people are attracted to these alternatives to marriage. Help your group to see how one popular view of God today—as a mean, joyless control-freak—is totally at variance with what we have learned about God the Provider in this session.

- There are times when it is hard to live according to God's design for sexual relationships—both as single and as married people—when the lifestyle of non-Christians around us appears freer and easier. Get your group to share what would help them not to stray from God's design at such times. Answers could include: regular Bible teaching and fellowship; help with applying Bible teaching; being reminded of the joy of the Christian life and the darkness of the non-Christian life; others committed to praying for you; being included in the church family; accountability to others; the advice of more mature Christians; the example and encouragement of godly married couples and godly single people, etc. (**Pastoral note:** Again, be aware that this question may expose painful issues for some in your group, so be ready to offer extra support and encouragement outside the session.)

EXPLORE MORE

	How has God provided for Christians?	What's the result for us?
1 Corinthians 1 v 7	He has enriched us in every way (v 5)	We do not lack any spiritual gift (v 7)
2 Corinthians 9 v 8	God's abounding grace can give us everything we need	We can abound in every good work
Ephesians 1 v 3	God has blessed us with every spiritual blessing in Christ	In Christ there's no spiritual blessing that is beyond us

	How has God provided for Christians?	What's the result for us?
Philippians 4 v 19	God can meet all our needs in Christ	In Christ there's no need that can't be met
2 Peter 1 v 3	God has given us everything we need for life and godliness	We can live a godly life

When we truly believe that this is how God provides for His people, we will be content, joyful, confident in our hope, unafraid and at peace, and seeking most of all to be godly and abounding in good works.

Genesis 3 v 1-7

GOD RULES

THE BIG IDEA

The root of all sin is a refusal to trust that God is the Ruler of our world, that His rule is good and that He always has our best interests at heart.

SUMMARY

Genesis chapter 3 is the account of humanity's disobedience to God (called the "Fall"). For the first time since creation, somebody questions whether God has really got it right. The question leads to doubt about the goodness of God's motives behind the command given to the man and woman. This doubt about God's word leads to disobedience, but disobedience leads to disaster, proving that God should have been trusted all along.

The challenge of this session is to trust God and His goodness even when we don't want to obey His word. Genesis 2 has provided us with a history of God's relationship with the human race from the very beginning. As we saw last session, He has always provided humanity with everything we need and much, much more. There is enough evidence of His generosity and goodness for us to put our trust in Him, even when there are aspects of His design that we find hard to understand or agree with.

Practical application here focuses on how to listen to God's word so that we will know it thoroughly, and how to avoid listening to Gods enemy, who tries to make us doubt His word. This is how we will grow in trusting obedience to God's rule in all areas of our lives.

OPTIONAL EXTRA

This activity aims to help people see that God's enemy is still speaking today and how we can be in danger of listening to that instead of God's word, just as Eve listened to the serpent and ignored God's command. Give your group a copy of a magazine or newspaper article (problem pages and comment columns provide useful material), or show a clip from a TV show or film, or play a popular song. Ask people to identify what is being said that opposes God's word and what makes it attractive to people today. Ask your group to share examples that they have come across recently. Powerful "enemy messages" today include: my personal happiness is my most important priority; life here and now is all that there is; there is great goodness inside everyone (or at least everyone who is "normal"); I have a right to control everything that happens to my body—including continuing or ending a pregnancy, and deciding when and how I die; no one has a right to judge anything that happens between consenting adults, etc.

GUIDANCE ON QUESTIONS

1. People might mention their significant relationships—parents, spouses, long-standing friends—or professionals, like a sports instructor, a doctor, a firefighter, etc. In relationships, trust is based on our previous history with that person. We trust people who have reliably acted in our best interests eg: have given us help when we needed it, have comforted us when we were upset, have respected us, have kept their promises to us, have kept confidences etc. Sometimes this includes things that we don't like, but which are good for us eg: challenging us about wrong behaviour or unwise decisions, or pushing us to do something we are afraid of. When it comes to professionals, we trust in the knowledge and expertise that they have and which we lack.

- **Do you only trust people you always agree with?** All children disagree with their parents at some point but it doesn't necessarily affect their trust.

- **Can you trust someone when you don't understand why they are taking a particular course of action?** You follow the instructions of an abseiling instructor even though they feel counter-intuitive, because he has knowledge and experience that you don't have. Similarly, patients will follow a doctor's instructions without necessarily understanding the reason for them.

Adam and Eve's lack of trust in God (Genesis 3) is inexcusable in the light of their previous experience of Him, as the generous Provider of all their needs (Genesis 2).

2. The serpent asks the question: "Did God really say…?"

- He starts his campaign to turn Adam and Eve away from God by making Eve doubt God's word.

- **Remember what we have learned about God's pattern for the different roles of men and women in marriage (Session 3: question 10). What else do you notice about the serpent's strategy here?** He chooses to speak to the woman, who was not the one directly instructed by God, rather than the man, who did receive God's command directly—see 2 v 15-17.

3. There's a subtle difference between God's command and Eve's recollection of it. She makes the prohibition much stronger—God didn't say they were not to touch the forbidden fruit. And she removes the positive emphases in God's permission: "You are free to eat from any tree in the garden…". It's as though this part of God's word was not really important to her—she appears to be focusing more on the negative command. This shows that already, in her view, God seems less generous and more restrictive than He is in reality.

4. First, he suggests that God has not told the truth, but has simply made an empty threat that He won't carry out. Secondly, he suggests that God's motives for making the prohibition are selfish ones—He wants to keep something good from Adam and Eve; namely, the knowledge of good and evil, which will make them "like God".

- At the beginning the serpent sowed doubt about whether Eve had heard or understood God's word correctly (v 1-3). But now he sows doubts about whether God's word is even worth listening to by suggesting that it is both untrue and nothing more than a means of repression or enslavement.

5. Eve looks at the fruit and finds it attractive. She also accepts what the serpent has suggested—that the fruit is "desirable for gaining wisdom". It is for these reasons that she decides to eat it.

6. God gave Adam a clear prohibition, and also a warning of the severe consequences of disobeying His command. He did this because He had the best interests of humanity at heart—humans should not and could not become like God in His authority and ultimate rule over creation, one aspect of which is to decide what is good and what is evil. Adam and Eve may not have understood these reasons for God's prohibition, but the central issue was whether they trusted God to do what was best for them. By eating the fruit, they showed that they preferred to accept the serpent's view of God, rather than take God Himself on trust.

• **How much were Adam and Eve to blame in failing to trust God? Or were they simply helpless victims of the serpent's deviousness?** This question applies to our relationship with God some of the things discussed in question 1 (Talkabout). Adam and Eve's experience of God was overwhelmingly good. He had lavishly provided for them everything they needed—whereas the serpent had never done anything for them. And as God was their Creator, they must have known that He had far greater knowledge, wisdom and power than they did. Who, then, were they to sit in judgment on God and His commands?

7. APPLY: This is an opportunity to air practical suggestions. Get people to share things they have found helpful in getting to know God's word better. Ideas include: giving priority to attendance at meetings where the Bible is taught; recommending helpful books; listening to Bible talks downloaded from the internet; using daily Bible-reading notes; meeting with another Christian specifically to discuss application or a question arising from Bible teaching that you've heard; joining with others to do a Bible course. The important point is that getting to know God's word better doesn't just happen to us—it involves investing time and effort. Aim for people in your group to have a plan of action that they can take from this session.

8. APPLY: Answers will vary from person to person. Answers are likely to include: the opinions of non-Christian friends and family; the values presented by TV and radio programmes, popular songs, films, magazines, newspaper columnists, internet sites etc; for students—the anti-Bible attitudes of teachers and fellow students in the academic world; for all of us—our thoughts and fantasies, telling us that things are not fair, that no one has it as hard as we do, that no one understands us, that something which God doesn't allow won't hurt us, etc.

• Most people struggle with one or two of the answers above. Taking action to stop listening to God's enemy may involve, say, no longer buying a favourite magazine; or making sure you meet up with a Christian friend after spending time with an influential non-Christian friend; or seeking help from a Christian leader to counter a college teacher's criticism of the Bible. Shape your discussion according to the struggles of the people in your group.

EXPLORE MORE

Isaiah 44 v 24 – 45 v 14: Isaiah's intention in this passage is to show that even the absolute head of the world's greatest superpower, Cyrus of Persia, is nothing but a pawn used by God, who alone has supreme power and authority to rule the universe.

God's power: God alone has created the universe (44 v 24, 45 v 12); He determines future events, vindicating His own prophets and humiliating false prophets (v 25); He controls where people live (v 26;); He can bring drought (v 27); He uses Cyrus to accomplish what He wants (v 28; 45 v 1, 13); He is the one who gives Cyrus his military success and his wealth (45 v 1-5); He creates light and darkness (v 7); He brings prosperity and disaster (v 7); He provides righteousness and salvation (v 8); He has created humanity (v 12); He turns world powers into slaves (v 14).

Cyrus: The mighty Persian emperor is a mere shepherd in God's eyes—nothing more elevated than a rough, menial servant (44 v 28); God is the one who directs what Cyrus does—he's like a puppet (45 v 1); and any success that Cyrus has achieved, he owes to God (v 2-3), even his honour (v 4); God makes Cyrus do just what He wants ie: rebuild Jerusalem and set God's people free (v 13).

The main lesson: There is nothing and no one like God.

The practical implications: Don't quarrel with God, question what He has done or try to tell Him what to do.

Jesus' view of God's authority: He came to do the will of His Father, not His own will (John 6 v 38); He obeyed His Father's commands (John 15 v 10); He was obedient to the point of dying on a cross (Philippians 2 v 8); and in the end, when He has destroyed every enemy, He will make Himself subject to His Father (1 Corinthians 15 v 28).

9. They make coverings of fig leaves to hide their nakedness (v 7), whereas previously they had felt no shame about being naked (2 v 25). Ironically, what the serpent promised the woman—"your eyes will be opened" (v 4)—comes true, but the experience is very different from what Adam and Eve must have expected.

10. God's order is overturned in three ways: 1. Mankind is now ruled by an animal (the serpent)—they follow what it tells them. 2. The woman, instead of helping the man to carry out God's instructions, leads him to do what God's enemy wants. 3. And the man, instead of leading the woman to fulfil God's commands, follows her into disobedience against Him.

11. APPLY: Allow people to share what is most relevant to them. You may need to start with an example of your own. Areas in which people often find it difficult to trust God may include: the safety and happiness of their children; financial problems; the salvation of non-Christian family and friends; that God has a good purpose in allowing pain, suffering and death; that it could be best to stay single or to remain in a difficult marriage, etc.

• In Genesis 3 we see that by following God's created order (male headship and humanity's rule over creation), Adam and Eve would have been saved from their disastrous course of action. And the shame and fear (more of this next session) unleashed by Adam and Eve's rebellion confirm that God's word truly had their best interests at heart. We, however, have even more history of God's faithfulness, generosity, wisdom and power in dealing with humanity. Emphasise that your Bible studies together are not simply an academic exercise, but the foundation on which trust in the perfect goodness of God can be built. The result should be a real and practical difference to your lives; for example, in the situations you have just discussed.

Genesis 3 v 8-24
GOD JUDGES

THE BIG IDEA

God is the perfect and only Ruler of our world, and so He is fair in His punishment of humans for rejecting His word and challenging His authority.

SUMMARY

In the second half of Genesis chapter 3 God responds decisively and immediately to Adam and Eve's disobedience. He places a curse on the serpent (the devil, who first sowed into Eve's mind doubt about God's word), on the woman (who followed the lead of a creature that she, with the man, was supposed to rule over), on the ground (until then a satisfying and fruitful resource for humans to work and feed from), and on the man (who failed to lead the woman in obedience to God's command, and instead followed her into sin). These curses changed the world from a perfect creation to one which, although it still reflects God's craftsmanship, is now blighted with shame, pain, conflict, drudgery and death. It is this judgment of God which explains why the world is now both wonderful and terrible.

God is fair in His judgment of the world and humanity like this because He is faithful to His word, and because He cannot allow humans to act as if they are like Himself with impunity. But true to His character, He also continues to show mercy, in the promise of a person who would destroy the devil and in providing a covering for Adam

and Eve to alleviate the shame they now felt at their physical nakedness.

This session confronts people with the fact that God will and must judge sin, because it ignores His word and challenges His unique authority. It seeks to show people the terrible consequences of human disobedience for our world and ourselves. But also to highlight that God is both fair and merciful, and to point ahead to Jesus Christ, who will rescue us from sin and its consequences.

OPTIONAL EXTRA

Divide your group into two teams and give each team the same list of subjects eg: the internet, medicine, the car. One group should list the good things that have come out of these technological developments, and the other should list the bad things. Get the groups to share their lists, perhaps alternating with each other, and see who has most ideas. This activity highlights the fact that since the Fall, our world, and especially human participation in our world, is both wonderful and terrible. This fact is explained by the events of Genesis 3—we have wonderful capacities because God created us, but also terrible capabilities because we are sinners and are under His curse (see question 9 below).

GUIDANCE ON QUESTIONS

1. A fair punishment will be proportionate to the crime (eg: it would be unfair to expel a child from school for forgetting their homework). It is those who are to blame who should be punished and not those who are innocent of wrongdoing—and one reason why people get unfairly punished is that humans are sometimes unable to find out for certain the truth about who is to blame for wrongdoing. Despite the fact that, in most countries, ignorance of the law is no defence, most people would find it unfair to be punished for something that they didn't know was wrong. This question prepares the ground for the issue of God's fairness in the punishment He imposed on Adam and Eve for disobeying His command. It will be clear that Adam and Eve knew that they were doing wrong and that they were to blame for their wrongdoing. What might be questioned by some in your group is whether God's punishment was proportionate to Adam and Eve's wrongdoing. The answer to this is tied up in their challenge to God's unique authority as Creator and sovereign Ruler of the universe.

2. Adam and Eve not only hide from each other (v 7), but also from God (v 8). They are now afraid of Him (v 10).

- In chapter 2 Adam had only good experiences of God, in the provision of the garden and of his wife, Eve. It seems that God spoke directly to Adam and spent time with him (v 15-17, 19, 21-22) without any suggestion of fear on Adam's part.

3. Notice how Adam avoids answering God's question directly. Instead he manages to blame both Eve and God—"The woman you put here with me". Eve too immediately shifts the responsibility away from herself by blaming the serpent for deceiving her. Adam seems to be suggesting that once the woman had given him the fruit, he couldn't help but eat it. Similarly, Eve seems to suggest that because the serpent had not told her the truth, she was the helpless victim of his wiles.

4. APPLY: Often our first reaction when challenged about a particular sin is to blame someone or something else—tiredness, financial stress, too much to do, upbringing, personality, other people (including other Christians) for making things hard for you, church leaders for not understanding what it's like to be you, God's word for being "difficult" and counter-cultural—even God, for not arranging your life or responding to what you want as you see fit. We need to be aware that we are increasingly living in a "blame culture", so we will all be tempted to "pass the buck".

- Like Adam and Eve, we become fearful of God—we lose our joy, we stop praying, we find God's word dry or remote from us.

5. The serpent: The serpent is to be the most cursed of all animals—perhaps referring to the fear and loathing that snakes seem to provoke worldwide (v 14). It will crawl on its belly— illustrating its degraded status as "lowest" form of life on land (v 14). There will be continual enmity between serpents and humanity (v 15). Serpents will attack humans and humans will slaughter serpents (but see also question 7 below).

Eve: Eve, and all women after her, will suffer increased pain in giving birth to children—perhaps not only physical pain but also the emotional stresses and griefs of raising children (v 16). Eve will seek to control her husband (the meaning of "desire" becomes clearer in Genesis 4 v 7, where the same word is used about Cain, who is in danger of being controlled by sin). But her husband will rule over her (v 16). This is the origin of "the battle of the sexes".

The ground: The ground is cursed as part of Adam's punishment. Instead of easily producing food for mankind, it will grow weeds that make agriculture a painful and exhausting drudgery (v 17).

Adam: As well as finding that the work he was created to do has become difficult and painful, Adam is also told that he will die and his body will return to dust (v 19).

6. Adam and Eve are banished from the Garden of Eden (v 23) and God ensures that it will be impossible for humanity to eat from the tree of life (v 24).

• The reason given here is that Adam and Eve have become like God and so must not be allowed to live forever. They have become like God specifically in "knowing good and evil". As mentioned in Session 3: question 5, "knowing good and evil" means deciding what is right and wrong. Humans, because they are creatures and not the Creator, are not qualified or equipped to do this, and the result of usurping God's rule in this way is unmitigated disaster. This is not a situation that God will allow to continue indefinitely, hence the exclusion of humanity from Eden and the tree of life.

7. The serpent is the devil, or Satan (see Revelation 12 v 9), and he will be crushed or destroyed by someone that he harms. Jesus became a human, the offspring of one of Eve's descendants—Hebrews 2 v 14 tells us He shared in our humanity. The devil, "who holds the power of death", tried to destroy Jesus at the cross, but the cross was in fact the way by which Jesus destroyed the devil—"by his death he [destroys] him who holds the power of death".

8. In verse 21 God provides a far better covering for Adam and Eve's nakedness— one which is costly because it involves the death of an animal.

• The covering of animal skins could not rid them of the shame, guilt and fear that they felt as a result of their disobedience to God; it was only external, covering their physical nakedness.)

• **How would God continue to provide like this for humanity?** (God gave His law to Israel, including regulations about sacrifices, priests and the tabernacle/temple, as a way of showing His people how sin must be covered and paid for. But again, this did not deal with the problem of the sinful human heart. These were "external regulations applying until the time of the new order"—Hebrews 9 v 10. The "new order" is the true atonement that only Jesus Christ can bring through His death on the cross—see Hebrews 10 v 12-14. But the purpose of these "external regulations" was to point humanity to Christ—see Hebrews 10 v 1a).

EXPLORE MORE

God's nature and character: His sovereign power (Psalm 50 v 1); His perfection (v 2); He isn't silent, but speaks (v 3, 7); He judges (v 4); He is righteous (v 6); He is utterly different from humanity, and has no needs (v 9,12,13).

Examples of wickedness: Answers include: merely paying lip service to God (v 16); hating God's word / ignoring it (v 17); following others into sin—"Everyone else does it" (v 18); using your tongue to hurt or damage others (v 19); hurting and damaging those closest to you (v

20). Highlight how commonplace these examples of wickedness are—they are not the gross sins and extreme lifestyles that most ordinary people can distance themselves from.

Why God must judge wickedness: If God doesn't judge wickedness, we will conclude that He is like us (v 21). God must punish sin in order to display His sovereignty, righteousness and "otherness". His judgment shows that He is utterly different from us—that He is, in fact, God, and we are not.

God's mercy: "The salvation of God" (v 23). At the time this psalm was written, Israel were supposed to follow God's law, including all the various sacrifices and offerings in the temple, which prepared the way for the future when God's salvation would be fully revealed in Jesus Christ (compare Titus 2 v 11-15 and Galatians 3 v 23-25).

How Psalm 50 fits with Genesis 1 – 3: God's nature and character—We saw God's sovereign power in the creation of the universe and His provision for humanity. We saw God's perfection in the fact that all He created was "good" and "very good". God spoke to the first man, giving him work, food, a command and addressing his need for a suitable helper. God judged the disobedience of Adam and Eve by cursing the serpent, the woman, the ground and the man. Wickedness—Adam and Eve both ignored God's word about the forbidden fruit. Eve followed the serpent in disobedience to God, and Adam followed Eve. Adam turned against Eve, blaming her for what had happened. Why God must judge sin—Adam and Eve were banished from Eden and cut off from the tree of life because God was determined to keep an unbridgeable difference between Himself and humanity (Genesis 3 v 22). God's mercy—God promised that one of the woman's descendants would destroy the serpent (ie: Satan), and God Himself provided a costly covering for the physical nakedness that was shaming Adam and Eve.

9. APPLY: As any wildlife programme will show, our world is both wonderful and terrible, and this contrast is also true of all human societies, cultures and civilisations. Our world is wonderful because God created it, and yet terrible because it is under God's curse as a punishment for sin. This explains why people are both capable of remarkable feats and yet incurably destructive of themselves, others and creation. Ask people to give examples of things they see in our world which illustrate this. Eg: marriage and family relationships—these are what most people long for and live for, yet they are one of the greatest causes of conflict, heartbreak and even murder; work—this is crucial to our sense of identity and wellbeing, and yet also a ball and chain that we long to be free of; religion—everywhere in the world religion has produced inspirational music, art, architecture and so on, yet also bitter conflicts and extreme violence.

10. APPLY: Allow people to share how they have or they might answer this question. Several different approaches can be taken. What we have seen in Genesis is that God had already proved Himself to be trustworthy and fair before Adam and Eve disobeyed Him. He provided them lavishly with everything they needed, He gave them great freedom, and He was clear about how they must obey Him and what would be the consequences of their disobedience. He was proved right by the immediate consequences of their misbehaviour—their shame, fear of Him and passing the blame. When we know what God is like, there is no reason to distrust His fairness. But most people have a totally wrong or very hazy idea of who He is and what He is like. This kind of question could be an opportunity to encourage someone to find out from the Bible what God is really like.

Genesis 4 v 1-26
GOD REMAINS

THE BIG IDEA
Now that humanity is in exile from Eden, sin escalates and the relationships between God, men, women and the world continue to deteriorate. But God does not abandon his creation. He remains involved as He works towards His plan of salvation.

SUMMARY
The story of Cain and Abel in Genesis 4 is very well known, but the chapter as a whole is generally over-shadowed by chapters 1 – 3. Given the break at the beginning of chapter 5 (where the text returns to Adam and then lists his descendants for a second time), we perhaps ought to see chapter 4 as completing the story of creation and Fall that was begun in chapters 2 – 3.

Chapter 4 makes us look back to the contrast of chapter 2, which showed us how incredible the world was under God's rule. Chapter 4, post-Fall, gives us a glimpse of how the world is under man's rule—awful. It is a chapter full of man's achievements—offerings, music, farming and industry. The tragedy is that none of these things re-unites humanity with God.

What's more, at every turn, human sin and its results grow. The world without God is a terrible place.

OPTIONAL EXTRA
The ongoing results of the Fall are that relationships break down and sin begins to escalate. Give your group a selection of magazines or newspapers and get them to spot stories that highlight the breakdown of relationships between individuals; husbands and wives; humanity and God; and humanity and the environment. Be sensitive to anyone in the group who is going through difficulties in an area such as marriage. Which of the stories represent some breakdown of relationship or behaviour that started off small but grew and is now out of control. There should be no problem with finding stories like this since the celebrity magazines thrive on them.

GUIDANCE ON QUESTIONS
1. There's nothing wrong with hobbies and this talkabout question might reveal some interests that nobody knew about. Some

may be modest about their achievements, especially in a Bible study. However, the discussion is designed to highlight our creativity and the variety of our gifts—all part of God's good world. By nature though, we are human and we tend to use those gifts selfishly. As we'll see, chapter 4 of Genesis is a very self-centred chapter.

2.

	What they offered	How God reacted
Abel	Fat portions from some firstborn of his flock	Looked with favour on Abel
Cain	Fruits of the soil	Didn't look with favour on Cain and asked him to do what was right

3. As it is presented here, the reason for Abel's sacrifice being acceptable is somewhat of a mystery. Note that there is no hint at this point that the lamb was the right thing and the vegetables (if that's what they were) were wrong. Later regulations for sacrifices allowed for both. However, Abel's acceptance reflects two Old Testament themes. 1. God's election—His choice of a younger brother, who would be a less significant person in that culture than a firstborn son (a theme that continues through Genesis). 2. The giving of the best in sacrifice—eg: the "fat portions" and the firstborn animals of Abel's flock—rather than any old thing (this is born out when God gives His laws about sacrifices in Exodus and Leviticus).

• Hebrews 11 v 4 tells us that it was by faith that Abel offered a better sacrifice than Cain did. It seems that the difference between the two brothers is that Abel had faith in God, whereas Cain did not. But we are still not told why Abel had faith (nor Noah or Abraham). But remember that faith is a gift from God (Ephesians 2 v 8).

(**NOTE**: For some of the reasons people have used to try and explain God's acceptance or rejection here: see *Salvation Begins*, p56.)

4. It seems that Cain thought God owed him acceptance merely because of the fact that he had made an offering. He felt he had already done enough to deserve God's favour, and that's why he was angry at God's lack of acceptance—he wasn't getting what he felt he deserved. Cain is repeating the sin of his father in thinking that he knows better than God—in this case, he knows better what the sacrifice should be!

• Cain wasn't willing to accept that it is God's right and privilege to choose who He will show favour to or not, and that obedience and trust in Him is what counts, not jumping religious hurdles. See 1 Samuel 15 v 22; Isaiah 1 v 11-17.

5. God gave Cain the choice to "do what is right", in which case God would accept him, or, if he didn't do what is right, he would be dominated by sin. Notice that at this stage Cain has not completely blown it. God is still willing to accept Cain, but he must do what is right.

• Doing right would mean agreeing with God's reason (whatever that was) for choosing not to show him favour. It would probably mean learning from his younger brother how to make an acceptable sacrifice to God. It undoubtedly meant that Cain would have to humble himself.

6. Cain's sinful offering leads at first to resentment, anger and sullenness. He stops listening to and putting into practice God's word and eventually murders Abel. Just as with Adam and Eve, the effects of the sin spread and grow. The ultimate result is, of course, judgment for Cain and further separation from both his family and God. Sin is always like this. A helpful illustration is that of dropping ink into clear water—the effect grows and grows until eventually all the water changes. Emphasise the way that sin drives a wedge between us and God. One of the first signs of this is a reluctance to listen to and obey God's word. It might start with the weight of a particular sin making us feel too guilty to read God's word, pray or go to church—the very things that would in fact remind us of God's grace!

7. Through God's mercy Cain's punishment is limited—it will not lead immediately to his death. Instead "God will be Cain's keeper in contrast with his failure to be his brother's keeper" (Andrew Reid). The "mark of Cain" is God's mark and it signifies His grace. It prompts us to look forward to other "marks" in the Bible—the marks on the doorposts at the time of the Passover (Exodus 12 v 7), the cross itself, and the seal of the Holy Spirit (Ephesians 1 v 13).

8. APPLY: The topic of worship is a complicated one, about which people can get quite emotional. However we all need to be challenged on the way that we approach God in worship. For some, it might be as simple as realising for the first time that "worship" means more than the singing in a church service. For others, it might be the challenge of being discerning about over-familiar language in some modern songs, when we are worshipping

together with God's people. All of us need to be more diligent in rejecting the world's view that worship is done to make me feel good. Living our lives to please God, and not ourselves or others, is a sacrifice—as it says in Romans 12 v 1. That means it's not easy and it will be costly.

EXPLORE MORE
Elijah's prayer differs hugely from the "worship" of the prophets of Baal. At heart, Elijah appeals to God to act because of who God is and for the glory of His name. The prophets, however, try to manipulate Baal into acting because of what they do (cutting, dancing, etc).

Our God is not a God to be manipulated. He doesn't respond because of who we are or what we have done. (This is just as well, given our sinful nature). God responds because of grace—His free gift to us, despite our behaviour towards Him, not because of it. It is all too easy to fall into this trap of expecting God to act because of our good behaviour, or making "deals" with Him ("I'll make a renewed effort in my prayers, Lord, if only you'll help me out of my current fix"). We fall into the trap of thinking that if we pray hard or long enough, or if we use certain words (grandiose words or even liturgy), that God will be duty bound to act. The antidote is to pray like Elijah—to get to know God better through His word, the Bible, and to appeal to His character, praying always for the glorifying of His name. Challenge your group (and yourself!) to start revolutionising the way they pray.

9. Jabal: He seemed to be a nomadic livestock farmer, presumably pioneering animal husbandry. **Jubal:** he was the artist of the family, and a pioneer in music. **Tubal-Cain:** he was the engineer and smith, pioneering in the area of technology.

10. None of the achievements is wrong, In fact they are great achievements that the human race relies on. However, none of them can bridge the gap that opened up between God and humanity at the Fall. You could think about how the commands given in the garden (to work the land, etc) and the punishment of the fall (the land will produce weeds) are found together in this chapter. We do see the purpose of the human race being worked out—in relationship with God, each other and the environment. However, at the same time, we see all those relationships being twisted and broken.

- Lamech's "boast" is a clear indication that, as human society, culture and industry grow, instead of the world becoming a better place, sin also escalates. We still see this in our society as scientific breakthroughs promise great things (that's Genesis 2) but also bring terrible misuse (that's Genesis 3 — 4).

NOTE: As humans, we are naturally sub-creators under God (to use a phrase that J.R.R. Tolkein liked) but we are so corrupted by sin that our achievements will never lead us back to God. In fact our achievements are likely to drive us away from God as we seek to make a name for ourselves; eg: the Tower of Babel in Genesis 11, which is the climactic event in the pre-Abraham part of Genesis. In modern terms we call this "humanism"— the idea that our universe is a closed system (there is no God) and any problems are products of the system (or of humans) and can therefore be solved by humans.

11. All of mankind is created to worship God; some will seek to worship the true and living God. Verse 26 brings a message of hope at the end of a chapter of despair and rottenness. Clearly some people begin to see the futility of their situation without God and start to seek Him. We also see hope in the birth of another son to Adam and Eve. We might have been left wondering what was going to happen to God's promise in Genesis 3 v 15—that a future descendant of the woman would strike the heel of the snake. Clearly that cannot now be either Abel or Cain. Seth provides new hope that God's promise is still on track.

12. APPLY: This final apply question sets up Session 7. We cannot bridge the gap back to God from our side, although men and women have always tried to since the days of Genesis 4. (You could think about how we still try to do that today eg: working hard to try and please God; religion and rituals; looking for God in the wrong places such as other religions or "spiritualities"; giving up on God and turning to other things (money, pleasure, drugs, relationship, career, travel etc) to find things that only God can provide.) The truth is that nothing will work. If the breakdown of our relationship with God is pictured as a gap between Him and us, we must conclude that the gap can only be bridged from God's side, and we need something or someone to be that bridge. How Jesus does this is the focus of Session 7. If your group have a good amount of Bible knowledge, you could discuss the following question:

- **How could you develop a discussion about the origin of the universe into an opportunity to explain the big picture of God's salvation plan in the rest of the Bible?** This question aims to get people thinking about creating an opportunity to share the gospel by using what they have learned in the sessions so far. It may be helpful to recommend a resource like *Two Ways to Live / The Choice We All Face*, which takes people from creation through our need and God's plan of salvation.

John 1 v 1-14
GOD STEPS IN

THE BIG IDEA
In the person of Christ, God has stepped into His creation to bring light and life, and re-establish the relationship He had with humanity that was lost as a result of the Fall.

SUMMARY
John starts his Gospel with a deliberate echo of Genesis 1. He is saying that "new creation" starts here. Jesus is given the title "the Word" and all of creation is attributed to Him. Again, this is a deliberate reminder of Genesis 1 and God's creation through His word alone. John is setting up his Gospel with this prologue to teach us that in Jesus we can see God and find life.

Since the Fall in Genesis 3, humanity has been cut off from God and the "tree of life". John tells us here that Jesus, the Word, brings light and life. Now we need not stumble around in the dark seeking God (eg: Genesis 4 v 26)—the light will help us find God. As a result of the Fall, we are subject to death—Jesus will reverse that to bring life.

There is fantastic news here. Jesus' incarnation is the beginning of the fulfilment of God's plan to reverse the effects of the Fall. This is ultimately achieved through Jesus' death and resurrection. Once again we have the opportunity to become part of God's family and enjoy a relationship of love and blessing with Him (just as Adam and Eve did) through Jesus. The sad part of this passage is that many (like Lamech in Genesis chapter 4) prefer the darkness of alienation from God.

OPTIONAL EXTRA

You might be doing this study in the middle of the summer, but why not get in the mood for this passage about the incarnation by finishing with a Christmas theme? You could eat Christmas food and swap presents. Secret Santa, anyone? You might want to swap some Christmas anecdotes and then look at the accounts of Jesus' birth in Luke and Matthew. John has written his Gospel in a slightly different way to teach us different but complementary things about Jesus' incarnation. Why do you think that might be?

GUIDANCE ON QUESTIONS

1. Here is a great opportunity to get some feedback on the previous six sessions. Jesus is not mentioned by name in Genesis 1 – 4. But Jesus is clearly the only person who is able to rule perfectly the way God intended (Session 2) and the only one who can crush the head of the snake (Session 4) or stand in the gap that has opened up between God and us as a result of the Fall.

2. John deliberately takes our minds back to Genesis 1 with the first three words of his Gospel. Here we are told of Jesus' involvement with creation. Together with Genesis 1 v 2, this establishes the fact that all three persons of the Trinity were present and active in creation. We are also reminded of the darkness that was present before creation, by reference to the darkness that now resides in men (v 5). There are many other connections that can be made, but don't dwell on them too

much—get into the text!

3. These verses are almost poetic, as with Genesis 1, and we may recognise a rhythm and familiarity, particularly from Christmas services. Jesus is eternal—He was with God in the beginning. Jesus is separate to God—He was with God—but He also was God. If you accept the statements in these verses—Jesus was with God and He was God—you have to believe in the Trinity. We see that each member of the Trinity was present at and active in creation. That means that the whole of the Trinity pre-existed creation ie: they are all eternal.

4. Everything was made through Jesus and, to emphasise this, John repeats it the other way around—nothing was made without Him. Jesus brings life to all things. This is not a contradiction of Genesis 2, where God breathes into man's nostrils and gives him life. It is the same event shown from a different angle.

5. Jesus also brings light into the world. "Light" will be an important idea in John's Gospel (compare 8 v 12). Right here at the beginning, John says that the life Jesus brings is going to be light for all. We will be able to see true life again. The same Jesus that gave life at creation has come into the world to bring life again. That is the light that John wants to switch on. Verse 3 reminds us that many people are completely indifferent to or ignorant of that light.

EXPLORE MORE

Beware of getting side-tracked into trying to explain the mystery of God's tri-unity. The important point is that the Bible clearly ascribes the power, nature and character of the one true God (Deuteronomy 6 v 4) to three Persons—Father, Son (Jesus) and Holy Spirit. We might not fully understand it but we should trust what God's word tells us.

6. APPLY: It is important to believe that Jesus was both fully God and fully human. He did not become part-human and part-God. He had the full complement of characteristics of both God and man. Many of us restate our belief in this every time we say a creed in church. This belief sets Christianity apart from all other religions, cults and sects. It is an important difference and the question of Jesus' identity is a good test to see if another group's views are biblical or not. More personally, we must also understand that our salvation could not be achieved unless Jesus is both fully divine and human in nature. Only He could stand in the dock on our behalf and sit at the judge's bench at the same time.

7. John clearly came as a witness. It is mentioned twice (v 7, 8). His role as a witness was to testify about Jesus so that people might believe in Him. In this section, John (the Gospel writer) makes it clear that John the Baptist's testimony is for everyone ("all men") and the true light (Jesus) comes for everyone ("every man"). Later on in John's Gospel there will be a lot of rejection of Jesus but the offer of light and life is there for all. Just as Adam and Eve rejected God's rule at the first creation, so many will reject this free offer of life to all as Jesus brings it.

8. The two reactions are acceptance or rejection of Jesus, God's living Word. Just as Adam and Eve chose to reject God's word in the Garden of Eden, so people would do the same to Jesus, and indeed, still do. It is a tragedy that the Fall has carried us so far from God that the world cannot even recognise its own Maker. As Creator, Jesus

has a right of ownership and rule over His creation, but even His own do not receive him (v 10-11).

• We become children of God when we "receive" Jesus and believe in His name (v 12), but notice that it is God who gives us new birth as one of His children ("he gave the right", v 12; "born of God", v 13). This is not something we can do for ourselves.

• This question allows people to reflect on the amazing privilege of becoming a child of God, with all the implications of a radically new and different relationship with God, who is now our Father. See also Romans 8 v 9-17.

9. Jesus has stepped into our world; He has become flesh (ie: human). For a short while God Himself came and lived among us. The word translated "made his dwelling" is literally "tabernacled". The tabernacle was the temporary temple—in fact an elaborate cloth tent—that the people of Israel took with them on their wilderness wanderings before entering the promised land. It was God's tent, where He used to meet with His people. Jesus temporarily made His home among us.

• By literally camping among us for a short while, Jesus has now become the way we can meet God. One feature of the original Old Testament tabernacle was that God's glory would descend and fill it. Moses, who used to talk with God, would come out with his face shining because of God's glory. Now, says John, that very same glory is on display in Jesus.

10. APPLY: To recognise Jesus means to make sure that we have correctly understood the Jesus of the Gospels and that we are not believing in a made-up version of Jesus. Anything less than Jesus our Creator, God made flesh, life-bringer, and part of the Trinity is not the Jesus that John is talking about.

It is not enough just to recognise Jesus for who He really is. Jesus' offer of life is made so that people will receive Him too. This means accepting Jesus as Saviour and Lord. In "Genesis terms", this means a re-establishment of the relationship that God had with Adam and Eve, but this time between us and Christ. And the really good news is that although we have to acknowledge our sin and shame (just like Adam and Eve), that sin is already dealt with. This relationship looks forward to a perfect new creation in heaven, rather than back to the first creation in Eden, that has now been spoiled. Below is a useful (though not comprehensive) checklist to help you answer this question about yourself or another person:

- How can you be confident of being saved from judgment?

- What has changed in the way you live since you came to recognise and receive Jesus?

- What is your attitude to the teaching of Jesus (both in His own words and the words of His apostles)?

- How has your relationship with God changed?

- How has your view of yourself changed?

- What do you now understand about your sin?

- What are you most looking forward to in the future?

Appendix
CREATION AND EVOLUTION

It is a fact that true Christians who hold the Bible to be the infallible word of God disagree about how or whether the teaching of Genesis chapters 1 and 2 can be reconciled with the theory of evolution. This presents a problem for any Bible-study guide covering these chapters. The debate cannot be ignored but, if allowed to dominate, there is a danger that the vast amount of other profitable teaching, understanding and application found in these chapters will be overlooked.

So it's vital to establish early in these sessions an understanding of this debate that recognises legitimate differences between genuine Christians, acknowledges the problems resulting from each position and defines the boundaries beyond which a Bible-believing Christian cannot go. And we should also set out some guiding principles for discussing these issues.

A. DIFFERENT VIEWS
Broadly speaking, Bible-believing Christians hold one of two views about what the Bible intends to teach us about creation. Both views give rise to problems.

1. WHO AND HOW
Those who advocate this position believe that the Bible tells us both who created the universe and how that was done. In other words, the events described in Genesis 1 should be taken more or less

literally (though there are differences of opinion over *how* literally eg: whether six days = six 24-hour periods or not.)

Problem: The accepted mass of scientific evidence in biology, geology and astronomy does not seem to fit this reading of the Genesis account, nor the timescale that it suggests. People who hold to this view can be taken up with seeking elaborate Bible-based explanations for these discrepancies, with variable success.

2. WHO, BUT NOT HOW
This group suggests that the Bible doesn't aim to tell us **how** the universe was created; its main preoccupation is to tell us **who** created the universe, and **why**. In other words, we can legitimately look outside the Bible to modern scientific theory for answers to questions about how the universe was created.

Problem: the mechanism of evolution doesn't appear to fit the Bible's view that creation was free of death until the Fall. Nor is evolutionary theory a comprehensive or even adequate account of how life came into existence and, in particular, of how humans came to be so different from animals.

B. AREAS OF UNITY

These are non-negotiables, which all Bible-believing Christians can be expected to believe:

- The Bible is the **infallible** word of God and stands above all other sources of knowledge. This means we look first to the Bible for knowledge and truth.

- The Bible is the **sufficient** word of God—it tells us everything that we need to know, although it does not tell us everything. This means that we do not go beyond what the Bible tells us by insisting that people take a position which the Bible does not clearly insist on.

- The Bible clearly tells us that God created the universe out of nothing.

C. GUIDING PRINCIPLES FOR DISAGREEMENT BETWEEN CHRISTIANS

- We can trust that even though there are questions that remain unanswered, God has given us in Scripture everything we need to be saved and to live a godly life (2 Timothy 3 v 16-17). Ultimately, this is what we must focus on.

- The Bible tells us (Romans 1) that it is the nature of sinners to suppress the truth about God. We need to be aware that this is how evolutionary theory is *used* by many unbelievers today—although it is a separate issue as to whether evolution represents the truth of how we came to be.

- None of us has perfect theological, linguistic, or scientific understanding. At some point we all have to exercise humility by admitting things that we do not know.

- The Bible tells us that it is wrong to judge another Christian on disputable matters (see Romans 14). Rather, we should "make every effort to do what leads to peace and to mutual edification" (v 19).

In your group you may have Christians who subscribe to both sides of the debate outlined above. You may also have new believers (or those who are new to these issues) who don't know what to think. Consider ahead of time how you will deal with questions, debates and disagreements arising in your group. On the one hand, you will need to make sure that a discussion of creation / evolution does not completely take over the sessions and eclipse the vital foundational teaching that these chapters have for us on the character and purposes of God, the nature of creation, and the realities of the our fallen human nature.

On the other hand, it is important not to ignore or dismiss people's questions. Above all, pray that your group's discussion will be an opportunity to grow in faith, love, and humility as well as understanding.

(Ideas taken from *Salvation Begins* by Andrew Reid, p14-20, available from The Good Book Company, www.thegoodbook.co.uk)

Also available in the Good Book Guide series...

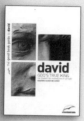

OLD TESTAMENT

Psalms: Work Songs
6 studies. ISBN: 9781905564675

Psalms: Soul Songs
6 studies. ISBN: 9781904889960

David: God's True King
6 studies. ISBN: 9781904889984

Ruth: Poverty and Plenty
4 studies. ISBN: 9781905564910

Ezekiel: The God of Glory
6 studies. ISBN: 9781904889274

Zechariah: God's Big Plan
6 studies. ISBN: 9781904889267

NEW TESTAMENT

Mark 1-8: The Coming King
10 studies. ISBN: 9781904889281

Mark 9-16: The Servant King
7 studies. ISBN: 9781904889519

Romans 1-5: God and You
6 studies. ISBN: 9781904889618

1 Thessalonians: Living to please God 7 studies. ISBN: 9781904889533

2 Timothy: Faithful to the end
7 studies. ISBN: 9781905564569

Hebrews: Consider Jesus
8 studies. ISBN: 9781906334420

1 Peter: Living in the real world
5 studies. ISBN: 9781904889496

1 John: How to be sure
7 studies. ISBN: 9781904889953

Revelation 2-3: A message from Jesus to the church today
7 studies. ISBN: 9781905564682

TOPICAL

Biblical Womanhood 9 studies.
ISBN: 9781904889076

Man of God 10 studies.
ISBN: 9781904889977

Women of Faith from the OT
8 studies. ISBN: 978190488952

Women of Faith from the NT
8 studies. ISBN: 9781905564460

The Holy Spirit 8 studies.
ISBN: 9781905564217

The Apostles' Creed 10 studies.
ISBN: 9781905564415

Contentment 6 studies.
ISBN: 9781905564668

Visit your friendly neighbourhood website to see the full range, and to download samples.
UK & Europe: www.thegoodbook.co.uk • N America: www.thegoodbook.com
Australia: www.thegoodbook.com.au • New Zealand: www.thegoodbook.co.nz

At The Good Book Company, we are dedicated to helping individual Christians and local churches grow. We believe that God's growth process always starts with hearing clearly what He has said to us through His timeless word—the Bible.

Ever since we started in 1991, we have been striving to produce resources that honour God in the way the Bible is used. We have grown to become an international provider of user-friendly resources to the Christian community, with believers of all backgrounds and denominations using our Bible studies, books, evangelistic resources, DVD-based courses and training events.

We want to equip ordinary Christians to live for Christ day by day, and churches to grow in their knowledge of God, their love for one another, and the effectiveness of their outreach. Call us to discuss your needs, or visit your friendly neighbourhood website for more information on the resources and services we provide.

UK & Europe: www.thegoodbook.co.uk
N America: www.thegoodbook.com
Australia: www.thegoodbook.com.au
New Zealand: www.thegoodbook.co.nz

UK & Europe: 0845 225 0880
N America: 866 244 2165
Australia: (02) 6100 4211
New Zealand (+64) 3 343 1990